Explore

Epicurus

Also by Gary W. Cross

Exploring the Way of Jesus
Exploring the Way of the Buddha
Exploring the Way of Lao Tzu
Exploring the Way of Epictetus

The Way of Sophia with Humps in Mind
Exploring Wisdom with Humps in Mind
Exploring a Good Life with Humps in Mind
Exploring the Mind – Discovering Humps and How they shape us

By Gary Cross and Cheryl Cross

The Way of Sophia circa 2017
Exploring a Way to a Good Life
Exploring Wisdom

Exploring the Way of

Epicurus

His destination, directions and strategies

Gary W. Cross

ISBN-13: 978-1481977685

ISBN-10: 1481977687

May 2017

Credit: Cover photograph by Marie-Lan Nguyen (2006) of a Bust of *Epicurus*, British Museum, Castellani Collection (GR 1873.8-20-726). Sourced from: *http://en.wikipedia.org/wiki/File:Epikouros_BM_1843.jpg*

Credit: Publishing logo by Sophie

Exploring the Way of Epicurus010717.docx

To my children and grandchildren, this book is first and foremost written for you.

So, we must attend to the things which bring happiness, since, if that is present, we have everything, and, if it is absent, all our actions are to have it.

CONTENTS

Preface

This book is part of the series *Ways of the World.* In this series, I explore the different ways of the world that have helped to shape my mind, and thus influence what I believe, say and do. The ways include religious, philosophical and secular ways. In particular, my aim is to seek to understand the way of the founder of each way.

In this book, my aim is to share with you the results of my explorations into the way of *Epicurus*[a].

The structure of this book

A way should tell us about: the destination that it leads to, any problems that may interfere with us reaching the destination, directions that will help us to reach the destination, and strategies that will assist us to overcome these problems and help us to successfully follow the directions. So in the first chapter my aim is to share with you what I discovered to be the destination that *Epicurus* suggests we all seek. Next, I present the problems that *Epicurus* suggests impedes our getting to the destination. Next, I present the directions that *Epicurus* offers to help us to reach the destination. And finally, I present the strategies that *Epicurus* offers to help us to overcome these problems and to successfully follow his directions.

A collection of flowers

As well as telling the results of my explorations in my words, I also try to have *Epicurus* speak for himself so that you too may explore the way of *Epicurus*. Thus, this book is primarily an

---

[a] *Epicurus* (342 – 270 BCE) was born in Samos, an island in the East Aegean Sea that was an Athenian colony. In Athens, he established a philosophical school and community based in his home and garden. After his death, philosophical schools following his philosophy (known as Epicureanism) spread throughout the Greek and Roman Empires.

anthology[a] - which literarily means it is a collection of flowers. In this case, the flowers are the quotations that I have gathered from the gardens (or works) of *Epicurus*. *Epicurus* wrote many books, letters and maxims - however little remains of his works with only three of *Epicurus'* letters still existing in their entirety. These three letters are found in Diogenes Laertius'[b] *Lives of the Philosophers*[c] which also has a collection of *Epicurus'* maxims[d]. It is from Diogenes Laertius' book that I sourced most of my quotations. Importantly, Laertius chose these three letters from the many then available to him because 'in these all of his philosophy is abridged'[e]. The next source that I gathered quotations from is the letters of Seneca[f] in which he often quoted *Epicurus*. The third source that I gathered quotations from is a collection of *Epicurus' maxims* rediscovered in the Vatican in 1888[g].

---

[a] *Anthology* comes from the Greek words *anthos* (blossom, flower) and *logia* (collection, gathering). Thus, *anthology* literary means 'a collection of flowers'.

[b] Little is known for certain of Diogenes Laertius other than he was the author of *Lives of the Philosophers* which is a ten volume set of books covering Greek philosophers from Thales to *Epicurus*. He probably lived in the third century CE; almost certainly lived in the then Western Roman Empire where Greek was the main language (*Lives of the Philosophers* was written in Greek); and possible lived in the province of Bithynia which is in modern day Turkey.

[c] The tenth volume of Diogenes Laertius *Lives of the Philosophers* contains *The Life of Epicurus* and includes the only three extant letters and a collection of maxims.

[d] Diogenes Laertius refers to them as τὰς Κυρίας αὐτοῦ δόξας, namely 'his authoritative thoughts'.

[e] Laertius 28

[f] Lucius Annaeus Seneca (ca. 4 BCE –65 CE) a Roman Stoic philosopher who was a tutor and advisor to the Emperor Nero. Although a Stoic, and thus considered in 'another team' to *Epicurus*, in his letters Seneca often quoted *Epicurus* 'for I am wont to cross over even into the enemy's camp...' Seneca was 'glad to repeat the distinguished words of *Epicurus*...'

[g] The collection of Epicurean maxims known as the *Vatican Sayings* was rediscovered in 1888 within a fourteenth-century Vatican manuscript.

Foreign flowers

Epicurus lived in ancient Greece between 342 to 270 BCE. Just as *Epicurus* clothed his body with the clothes of this period, so too did he clothe his thoughts with the language, words and concepts used at that time and place[a] - language, words and concepts very different to those we are now familiar with. So, when viewing the quotations be aware that they are from a remote time and place, and thus of course will look different, perhaps even seem strange or mysterious to us now (even when translated). Perhaps we need to try to imagine what they would look like if they originated in our time and place and clothed in our words and concepts.

A note on the translations

Diogenes Laertius' *Lives of the Philosophers* and *The Vatican Sayings* were written in an ancient form of Greek known as *Koine*[b] Greek which was the language used throughout the eastern Roman Empire for administration, trade and other general use. The quotations I present in this collection are my own translations[c] from the Greek versions of these texts available today[d].

---

[a] Imagine if *Epicurus* didn't use the language (ancient Greek), words and concepts that existed at that time and place – no one then would have understood what he was saying.

[b] *koine* (*koinos* common, shared in common; common to all people, public). Thus, *Koine* Greek was common Greek or the form of Greek used at the time (first century CE) for common use. *Epicurus* would have use a more ancient form of Greek current in the third and fourth centuries BCE.

[c] With frequent, and necessary, references to Koine Greek grammars and Greek-English Lexicons, in particular to the LSJ (Liddell, Scott, Jones) *Greek English Lexicon* (available at *http://www.perseus.tufts.edu*) and *The New Thayer's Greek-English Lexicon of the New Testament*.

To help ensure my translations were not too far 'off track' I constantly referred to the English translations by Hicks (1925), Inwood & Gerson (1994), Yonge (1853) and Saint-Andre (2010).

[d] Diogenes Laertius' *Lives of the Philosophers* from Robert Drew Hick (1925) sourced from: *http://www.perseus.tufts.edu/*; and *The Vatican Sayings* from Hermann Usener's (1887) *Epicurea* sourced from *http://www.monadnock.net/Epicurus /vatican-sayings.html#n4*

The quotations from Seneca (who wrote in Latin, the language of ancient Rome) I sourced from the translation by Richard M. Gummere[a].

Importantly it is often difficult to know exactly what an author meant, especially if the author is no longer around to ask! This is particularly a problem when the author is from a different or foreign group or culture and thus uses different words and concepts to construct what they want to say. For example, in translating most words there are many different meanings and nuances to choose from (just look up any dictionary for almost any word). The problem the translator has is to determine which meaning or nuance to use. And of course, the translator's own concepts, beliefs and desires influence their choice. Thus, when you read any translation you are exposed to not just the original author's concepts, beliefs and desires, but also those of the translator.

A note on the footnotes

In the footnotes, you will find the meanings and varied nuances for many words in the quotations. The footnotes help you to not only understand how I arrived at my translations, but they also allow you to better appreciate the richness of the original words and thus the richness of the original quotation. Also, from the footnotes you can choose the meaning or nuance that you think better suits the particular quotation and thus form your own translation! Importantly, I have tried to provide those meanings and nuances that existed at the time of *Epicurus*. So, if you wish to explore further a particular word or quotation, then the footnotes[b] will help you. For

---

[a] Lucius Annaeus Seneca. *Moral Epistles.* Translated by Richard M. Gummere. The Loeb Classical Library. Cambridge, Mass.: Harvard UP, 1917-25. 3 vols – sourced from:
http://www.stoics.com/seneca_epistles_book_1.html, book2 and book3.

[b] The footnotes consist of three parts: First, the Greek word found in the text. Next, I include the lexicon form of the word (unless the word is the lexicon form) and the various nuances and meanings of the lexicon form. Then finally, the grammatical form of the word (which I normally use in my translation).

example, referring to the footnotes you could explore the meaning of *Epicurus'*[a] name.

---

[a] ἐπίκουρος an assister, ally, helper; helping, assisting, aiding; mercenary troops

Acknowledgements

I have been very fortunate to have Cheryl's and Emily's help when writing this book. Despite hectic lives and many commitments, Cheryl and Emily still found time to help improve this book by providing comprehensive feedback which ranged from pointing out formatting, spelling and grammatical errors through to comments and discussions about the book in general.

This book would be very much the poorer without their assistance.

1

THE DESTINATION – happiness

The destination that *Epicurus* tells us to seek is *happiness*.

'So, we must attend to the things which bring happiness[a], since, if that is present, we have everything, and, if it is absent, all our actions are to have it.' [Laertius, 122][b]

And what is happiness? *Epicurus* tells us that happiness is having a healthy body and tranquil psyche, that is, we are happy when we are free from physical and mental pain.

"He who has an unwavering contemplation of these things will refer every choice and avoidance towards a healthy[c] body[d] and tranquil[e] psyche[f] seeing that this is the fulfilment of a blessed[g] life[h]. For all we do is for the sake of us having no pain[i] and no fear[j]...' [Laertius, 128]

---

[a] εὐδαιμονίαν (εὐδαιμονία good daemon, genius, lot or fortune; prosperity, good fortune, wealth, happiness) happiness

[b] The numbers refer to the position of the text in Laertius' book.

[c] ὑγίειαν (ὑγίεια health, soundness) healthy

[d] σώματος (σῶμα body, the body of a person; any material substance; the whole body of a thing) body

[e] ἀταραξίαν (ἀταραξία impassive, calm, tranquil) tranquil

[f] ψυχῆς (ψυχή psyche, breath, breath of life, vital force, the source of life, the life, the spirit, the soul, anima; that which is responsible for perception, thoughts, emotions, desires and affections; the mind) psyche

[g] μακαρίως (μακάριος blessed, happy, prosperous, fortunate) happy

[h] ζῆν (ζωη life, state of one filled with breath or vitality; existence; a way of life, a living, one's means of life) life

[i] ἀλγῶμεν (ἀλγέω to feel bodily pain, suffer; to feel pain of mind, to grieve) pain

[j] ταρβῶμεν (ταρβέω to be frightened, alarmed, terrified; to fear) fear

'...the (goal) is no pain[a] in the body[b] and no turmoil[c] in the psyche[d].' [Laertius, 131]

THE DESTINATION – in essence

Epicurus believes that the destination we all seek is happiness, which he equates with having a healthy body and tranquil mind, that is, a state free from physical and mental pain.

THE DESTINATION in essence: happiness, a state free from pain.

Note: As well as using the word εὐδαιμονίαν[e] for happiness, *Epicurus* also uses the word μακάριον[f]; and as well as using the words ἀταραξίαν[g] ψυχῆς[h] ('tranquil psyche') he also uses the word ἀτάραχον[i] ('peace of mind').

---

[a] ἀλγεῖν (ἀλγέω to feel bodily pain, suffer; to feel pain of mind, to grieve) feeling pain

[b] σῶμα body, the body of a person; any material substance; the whole body of a thing

[c] ταράττεσθαι (ταράσσω to agitate, to stir up trouble, turmoil, to takeaway calmness of mind, to make restless, to throw into disorder) turmoil

[d] ψυχήν (ψυχή psyche, breath, breath of life, vital force, the source of life, the life, the spirit, the soul, anima; that which is responsible for perception, thoughts, emotions, desires and affections) psyche

[e] εὐδαιμονίαν (εὐδαιμονία good daemon, genius, lot or fortune; prosperity, good fortune, wealth, happiness) happiness

[f] μακάριον (μακάριος blessed, happy, prosperous, fortunate) happiness

[g] ἀταραξίαν (ἀταραξία impassive, calm, tranquil) tranquil

[h] ψυχῆς (ψυχή psyche, breath, breath of life, vital force, the source of life, the life, the spirit, the soul, anima; that which is responsible for perception, thoughts, emotions, desires and affections; the mind) psyche

[i] ἀτάραχον (ἀτάρακτος no disturbance or commotion (of mind); not excited, calm, (mental) tranquillity, peace of mind) peace of mind

2

PROBLEMS – physical and mental pains

If happiness is a state free from physical and mental pain, then the obvious problem is the existence of pain! Pain is the antithesis of happiness.

Pain is the bad:
'...feeling pain[a] or being distressed[b], that is the bad[c].' [Laertius, Maxim X, 142]

Mental pains include fear of the gods, death and the fear of pain itself:
'...fears[d] of the mind[e], such as about celestial phenomena[f], and death[g], and pain[h]...' [Laertius, Maxim X, 142]

---

[a] ἀλγοῦν (ἀλγέω to feel bodily pain, suffer; to feel pain of mind, to grieve) feeling pain

[b] λυπούμενον (λυπέωto give pain to, to pain, distress, grieve, annoy; to be pained, grieved, distressed) being distressed

[c] κακόν (κακός bad, of a bad nature, not as it ought to be; base, wrong; troublesome, destructive, evil; worthless) bad

[d] φόβους (φόβος fear, dread, terror) fear

[e] διανοίας (διάνοια mind, the mind as the faculty of understanding, feelings, desire; thought, intention, purpose) mind

[f] μετεώρων (μετέωρος raised from the ground, in mid-air, high in the air; things in heaven above; celestial phenomena, astronomical and meteorological phenomena) celestial phenomena (such as lightening, thunder, rain, the stars, sun, moon and planets)

[g] θανάτου (θάνατος death) death

[h] ἀλγηδόνων (ἀλγηδών a sense of pain, pain, suffering) pain

Fear of the gods:
The first fear of the mind that *Epicurus* highlights is our fear that
the gods will do things that harm us, such as causing harmful
celestial phenomena (for example lightening).

'In addition to all of this there is need to thoroughly understand,
that the most powerful[a] disturbance[b] in the human[c] psyche[d] arises
through the belief[e] that the happy[f] and eternal[g] (i.e. the gods), do
things and are responsible for things contrary to[h] their will[i]...'
[Laertius, 81]

---

[a] κυριώτατος (κύριος master, lord, having power or authority over;
authoritative, most powerful) most powerful

[b] τάραχος commotion, stir, disturbance, disorder, turmoil, anxiety

[c] ἀνθρωπίναις (ἀνθρώπινος of, from, or belong to man, human; human)
human

[d] ψυχαῖς (ψυχή psyche, breath, breath of life, vital force, the source of
life, the life, the spirit, the soul, anima; that which is responsible for
perception, thoughts, emotions, desires and affections; the mind) psyche

[e] δοξάζειν (δοξάζω to think, suppose, be of the opinion, to believe,
imagine; praise, magnify, celebrate) to believe

[f] μακάρια (μακάριος blessed, happy, prosperous, fortunate) happy

[g] ἄφθαρτα (ἄφθαρτος eternal, uncorrupted, undecaying) eternal

[h] ὑπεναντίας (ὑπεναντίος opposite to, set over against, contrary to,
opposed to) contrary to

[i] βουλήσεις (βούλησις will, intention, purpose, desire) will

Fear of death:
The second fear of the mind that *Epicurus* highlights is our fear of death, which he suggests we have because of what we have been told about death, and because we fear the possibility of nothingness.

'And in the eternal[a] (i.e. death) we always expect[b] or suspect[c] fearful[d] things 'according to myths[e] and also this, the lack of sensation[f] in death[g] we fear[h]...' [Laertius, 81 continued]

Fear of pain itself
The third fear that *Epicurus* highlights is our fear of pain itself:

'...fears[i] of the mind[j], such as about ... pain[k]...' [Laertius, Maxim X, 142]

---

[a] αἰώνιον (αἰώνιος lasting for an age, everlasting, eternal) eternal

[b] προσδοκᾶν (προσδοκάω expect, think, suppose) expect

[c] ὑποπτεύειν (ὑποπτεύω to be suspicious, to suspect, guess, suppose) suspect

[d] δεινόν (δεινός fearful, terrible, dire) fearful

[e] μύθους (μῦθος myth, word, speech, story, tale) myth

[f] ἀναισθησίαν (ἀναισθησία lack of sensation, insensibility, no feeling or perception) lack of sensation

[g] τεθνάναι (θνήσκω to die, be dying, perish) death

[h] φοβουμένους (φοβέωto put to flight, terrify, alarm, frighten; to fear, be afraid, to be struck with fear) fearing

[i] φόβους (φόβος fear, dread, terror) fear

[j] διανοίας (διάνοια mind, the mind as the faculty of understanding, feelings, desire; thought, intention, purpose) mind

[k] ἀλγηδόνων (ἀλγηδών a sense of pain, pain, suffering) pain

Pains of want:
Another pain that *Epicurus* highlights is our 'pain[a] due to want[b]' [Laertius, Maxim 21], that is the pains we feel when we have unfulfilled desires.

Epicurus also tells us of 'need(s)[c] involving anxious[d] circumstances[e]' [Laertius, Maxim X 146], that is the pains we feel from trying to fulfil desires that involve anxiety when trying to satisfy them.

THE PROBLEMS that *Epicurus* identified – in essence

Epicurus tells us that the obstacle to happiness is pain – physical and mental, and that mental pains include:
 : Fear of the gods;
 : Fear of death;
 : Fear of pain itself;
 : Pains of want.

The problem in essence: pain

'And tranquillity[f] is to be released from all this…' [Laertius, 82]

---

[a] ἀλγοῦν (ἀλγέω to feel bodily pain, suffer; to feel pain of mind, to grieve) to pain

[b] ἔνδειαν (ἔνδεια want, need, lack, deficiency, defect) want

[c] προσδεῖται (προσδέω to want besides, need in addition; to be in want of, stand in need of; bind on or to, attach) need

[d] ἀγῶνας (ἀγών a gathering, a place of assembly; a place of contest, a contest; mental struggle, anxiety) anxiety

[e] πραγμάτων (πρᾶγμα deed, act, that which has been done; a matter, affair; thing of consequence, importance; circumstances, affairs) circumstances

[f] ἀταραξία impassive, calm, tranquil

3

EPICURUS' DIRECTIONS – be a philosopher

How do we overcome the problems and reach our destination? That is, how do we gain happiness; how do we achieve a healthy body and tranquil psyche; how do we reduce physical and mental pain? *Epicurus* tells us that it is by being a philosopher (a lover of wisdom) that we will determine the answers to these questions and thus determine how to reach our destination.

'Let not the young delay to philosophize[a]; and let not the old weary of philosophizing: for it is never too early nor too late for the psyche[b] to be healthy[c]. And the ones saying that it is not yet time to philosophize, or the time has passed by are like the ones saying of happiness[d], not yet is the time for it, or no longer is the time for it.' [Laertius, 122]

'If you would enjoy real freedom, you must be the slave of philosophy.' [Seneca, 8]

---

[a] φιλοσοφεῖν (φιλοσοφέω to philosophize, to love wisdom, knowledge) to philosophize

[b] ψυχήν (ψυχή psyche, breath, breath of life, vital force, the source of life, the life, the spirit, the soul, anima; that which is responsible for perception, thoughts, emotions, desires and affections; the mind) psyche

[c] ὑγιαῖνον (ὑγιαίνω to be sound, healthy) to be healthy

[d] εὐδαιμονίαν (εὐδαιμονία good daemon, genius, lot or fortune; prosperity, good fortune, wealth, happiness) happiness

Laertius tells us that *Epicurus* saw philosophy as being composed of three parts, *The Canon, Physics* and *Ethics*:

'...some few preliminary remarks upon his division of philosophy[a]. It is divided into three parts, *The Canon*[b], *Physics*[c], *Ethics*[d].' [Laertius, 29]

And so now, I will briefly explore these three parts of *Epicurus'* philosophy with the aim of seeing how these provide the basis for his directions to happiness.

---

[a] φιλοσοφίας (φιλοσοφία philosophy; love of wisdom) philosophy
[b] κανονικὸν (κανών canon; a straight rod, staff, stick or bar, esp. to keep a thing straight; a measuring rod, rule; an established principle; a rule or standard, a principle or law of investigating, judging, living, acting; logic) canon
[c] φυσικὸν (φυσικός physics; of or produced by nature, natural, of or to do with physical things) physics
[d] ἠθικόν (ἠθικός ethics; of or for morals, ethical, moral) ethics

¤ *The Canon*

Laertius tells us that the Canon covers the basics of *Epicurus'* philosophy:

'The canon has the methods[a] to the treatise[b]... They say this is about the means of judging[c], first principles[d] and elementary[e]...' [Laertius, 30]

Sensations, preconceptions and feelings

Central to *Epicurus'* canon is that sensations, preconceptions and our feelings should form the basis of our truths, judgements, and beliefs - as Laertius goes on to tell us:

'In *The Canon Epicurus* states that the criteria[f] of truth[g] are sensations[h] and preconceptions[i] and feelings[j];' [Laertius, 31]

---

[a] ἐφόδους (ἔφοδος approach, means of approach, method of reasoning) methods

[b] πραγματείαν (πραγματεία prosecution of business; occupation, business; treatment of a subject, philosophical argument or treatise) treatise

[c] κριτηρίου (κριτήριον the means or rule of judging, a criterion, standard, test) the means of judging

[d] ἀρχῆς (ἀρχή beginning, origin, first cause; the person or thing that commences, the first person or thing in a series; first principle, element) first principles

[e] στοιχειωτικόν (στοιχειωτικός elementary, the first thing from which others follow, first principles) elementary

[f] κριτήρια (κριτήριον the means or rule of judging, a criterion, standard, test) criteria

[g] ἀληθείας (ἀλήθεια truth – as opposed to a lie or mere appearance) truth

[h] αἰσθήσει (αἴσθησις sense perception, sensation, the senses; perception, not only by the senses but also by the intellect, cognition) sensations

[i] προλήψεις (πρόληψις before taking hold, before conception, preconception, mental picture; conception) preconceptions

[j] πάθη (πάθος that which happens to a person or thing, experience; passion, feeling, emotion) feelings

On Sensations

Epicurus tells us that our sensations (the information we gain from our senses such as our eyes and ears) are irrefutable and should form the primary source of our evidence that we use when reasoning and forming judgements.

'Nothing is able to refute[a] them (sensations).' [Laertius, 31]

'... indeed reason[b] can not (refute them), for all reason depends on sensations[c]. And nor does one (sensation) depend on the other, for we attend to all. And the reality of separate perceptions[d] confirms the truth of our sensations. But seeing[e] and hearing[f] stand as support[g] like feeling pain[h]: and hence concerning the unknown[i] it is necessary to interpret it from the known[j]. For all our thoughts[k]

---

[a] διελέγξαι (διελέγχω refute, convict, expose, dispute) refute

[b] λόγος a word, what one has said; computation, reckoning, calculating, consideration; thinking, reasoning, reason; explanation, cause, ground, proposition, principle, law

[c] αἰσθήσεων (αἴσθησις sense perception,, sensation, the senses; perception, not only by the senses but also by the intellect, cognition) sensations

[d] ἐπαισθήματα (ἐπαίσθημα perception Perceptions

[e] ὁρᾶν (ὁράω to see, look, observe, to see with the eyes; to see with the mind, to perceive, know) to see

[f] ἀκούειν (ἀκούω to hear, to listen to, to attend to; to understand, perceive the sense of what is said) to hear

[g] ὑφέστηκε (ὑφίστημι place or stand under, support) stand as support

[h] ἀλγεῖν (ἀλγέω to feel bodily pain, suffer; to feel pain of mind, to grieve) feeling pain

[i] ἀδήλων (ἄδηλος not manifest, not seen or known, unknown, obscure, uncertain) unknown

[j] φαινομένων (φαίνω to bring to light, to shed light, to make clear, to make known) to make known

[k] ἐπίνοιαι (ἐπίνοια thought, purpose, notion) thoughts

derive from sensations, by experience[a] and analogy[b] and similarity[c] and composition[d], and anything bought together with reason[e].'
[Laertius, 32]

'...the sensations[f] provide all the evidence, according to which of necessity reason[g] forms a judgement[h] about the unknown[i].'
[Laertius, 39]

On Preconceptions

Epicurus' use the word or concept *preconception* is different to our use today. Today a preconception is an idea or opinion formed in advanced of adequate knowledge (hardly a basis for our judgements, etc.) whereas *Epicurus'* use of preconception seems to be closer to what we would call memories, in particular memories of sensations (which, assuming our memories are good, are a reasonable basis for our judgements, etc.).

---

[a] περίπτωσιν (περίπτωσις encountering, experience, actual contact) experience
[b] ἀναλογίαν (ἀναλογία analogy, proportion, equivalent to, resembling) analogy
[c] ὁμοιότητα (ὁμοιότης likeness, resemblance, similarity) similarity
[d] σύνθεσιν (σύνθεσις a putting together, composition, combination; combination of parts to form a whole) composition
[e] λογισμοῦ (a reckoning, computation, reason, reasoning power) reason
[f] αἴσθησις sense perception, sensation, the senses; perception, not only by the senses but also by the intellect, cognition
[g] λογισμῷ (λογισμός reason, reasoning power; reckoning, calculation, computation, consideration) reason
[h] τεκμαίρεσθαι (τεκμαίρομαι decree, appoint, ordain, judge, forms a judgement or conjecture) forms a judgement
[i] ἄδηλον (ἄδηλος unknown, unseen, obscure) unknown

'Preconception[a] they say is a kind of understanding[b] or right opinion[c] or thought[d] or general stored[e] idea[f], that is a memory[g] of a frequently seen external[h] (object), such as such a one is a man[i] – for as soon as the word man is uttered, the preconception and the form[j] of his is perceived by the mind[k] (according to) preceding sensations.' [Laertius, 33]

On Feelings
When referring to feelings *Epicurus* refers in particular to feelings of pleasure and pain. If feelings of pleasure and pain are seen as internal sensations (that is, information we gain from

---

[a] πρόληψιν (πρόληψις before taking hold, before conception, preconception, mental picture; conception) preconception

[b] κατάληψιν (κατάληψις a thorough taking hold, receiving, or seizing; direct apprehension of an object by the mind, understanding, perception) understanding

[c] δόξαν (δόξα opinion, judgement, view, a notion, belief, thought, expectation; splendour, brightness, magnificence, excellence, majesty, exalted) opinion

[d] ἔννοιαν (ἔννοια a thought, conception, act of thinking, reflection) thought

[e] ἐναποκειμένην (ἐναπόκειμαι stored) stored

[f] νόησιν (νόησις understanding, idea, concept) idea

[g] μνήμην (μνήμη mneme, remembrance, memory) memory

[h] ἔξωθεν from without, outward, external

[i] ἄνθρωπος a human being, whether male or female, man (generic term)

[j] τύπος a mark or figure formed by a blow, print, impression, form

[k] νοεῖται (νοέω to perceive with the mind, to understand, ponder, consider; observe, notice)

internal senses) then, as *Epicurus* states 'sensations provide all the evidence…'

'Feelings[a] they say are two: pleasure[b] and pain[c]…' [Laertius, 34]

'Hence, we must attend to present feelings[d] (and experiences)[e], those we share in common[f] with the public[g] and those privately[h] one's own[i], and all of these (present feelings and experiences) according to each of the clear[j] criteria[k]. For if we attend[l] to these, we will correctly explain fully how anxiety[m] and fear[n] came into being, and we can be set free (from them), by accounting for the

---

[a] πάθη (πάθος that which happens to a person or thing, experience; passion, feeling, emotion) feelings

[b] ἡδονὴν (ἡδονή enjoyment, pleasure, delight; desire for pleasure; desire for pleasure) pleasure

[c] ἀλγηδόνα (ἀλγηδών a sense of pain, pain, suffering) pain

[d] πάθεσι (πάθος that which happens to a person or thing, experience; passion, feeling, emotion) feelings

[e] perhaps *Epicurus* is using this meaning of the word πάθεσι

[f] κοινόν common, share in common; common to all the people, public, general; of common origin; the state, public authorities; ordinary, usual) share in common

[g] κοιναῖς (κοινός common, share in common; common to all the people, public, general; of common origin; the state, public authorities; ordinary, usual) public

[h] ἴδιον (ἴδιος one's own, pertaining to oneself, private, not public, personal; separate, distinct) private

[i] ἰδίαις (ἴδιος one's own, pertaining to oneself, private, not public, personal; separate, distinct) one's own

[j] ἐναργεία (ἐνάργεια clearness, distinctness, vividness; clear and distinct perception, clear view)

[k] κριτηρίων (κριτήριον criterion, means for judging or trying anything, the rule by which one judges, standard) criteria

[l] προσέχωμεν (προσέχω to bring near; to turn to or towards; to turn one's mind to, attend to, be attentive; to apply one's self to)

[m] τάραχος commotion, stir, disturbance, disorder, turmoil, anxiety

[n] φόβος fear, dread, terror

celestial phenomena[a] and the remaining[b] which always befalls[c] us, and which greatly fears[d] others extremely.' [Laertius, 82]

Reason

While sensations, preconceptions and feelings provide the raw materials, *Epicurus* tells us that reason is the tool that we use on these raw materials to shape our philosophy.

'... it is calm and collected[e] reasoning[f], and searching out[g] the grounds[h] of every choice[i] and avoidance[j], and banishing those beliefs[k] through which the greatest turmoils[l] take possession of the psyche[m].' [Laertius, 131-132]

---

[a] μετεώρων (μετέωρος raised from the ground, in mid-air, high in the air; things in heaven above; celestial phenomena, astronomical and meteorological phenomena) celestial phenomena (such as lightening, thunder, rain, the stars, sun, moon and planets)

[b] λοιπῶν (λοιπός the remaining, remaining over, the rest) remaining

[c] παρεμπιπτόντων (παρεμπίπτω to fall in or sides; creep in, effect and entrance; to be inserted; intervene; occur, present itself, happen; befall) befalls

[d] φοβεῖ (φοβέω to put to flight, terrify, alarm, frighten; to fear, be afraid, to be struck with fear) fear

[e] νήφων to be sober, to be calm and collected, dispassionate, circumspect

[f] λογισμός reason, reasoning power; reckoning, calculation, computation, consideration

[g] ἐξερευνῶν (ἐξερευνάω search out or examine anxiously and diligently) searching out

[h] αἰτίας (αἰτία responsibility; cause, reason, grounds; charge of crime) grounds

[i] αἱρέσεως (αἵρεσις act of taking, capturing; choice, that which is chosen) choice

[j] φυγῆς (φυγή flight or escape, aversion, avoidance) avoidance

[k] δόξας (δόξα opinion, judgement, view, a notion, belief, thought, expectation; splendour, brightness, magnificence, excellence, majesty, exalted) beliefs

[l] θόρυβος a loud confused noise, tumult, uproar, turmoil, confusion

[m] ψυχάς (ψυχή psyche, breath, breath of life, vital force, the source of life, the life, the spirit, the soul, anima; that which is responsible for perception, thoughts, emotions, desires and affections; the mind) psyche

'Chance[a] seldom effects the wise[b]; for his greatest and highest (matters) have been managed by[c], are managed by, and will be managed by reason[d] during the bewildering[e] period[f] of life[g].' [Laertius, Maxims XVI, 144]

Epicurus' Canon in essence

Epicurus suggests that:

: Sensations, preconceptions (the memories of sensations) and the feelings of pleasure and pain should be the evidence upon which all our judgements and beliefs are based; and

: Reason should be the tool used to determine our judgements and beliefs.

---

[a] τύχη chance, luck, good or bad fortune; the act of a god - Fortune, Fate

[b] σοφῷ (σοφός wise; wise in a practical sense, skilled, expert; clever) wise

[c] διῴκηκε (διοικέω to keep house; control, manage, administer; provide, furnish) have been managed by

[d] λογισμός reason, reasoning power; reckoning, calculation, computation, consideration

[e] συνεχῆ (συγχέω to pour together, commingle; confound, bewilder, perplex, trouble) bewildering

[f] χρόνον (χρόνος time; period; lifetime, age) period

[g] βίου (βίος the period or course of life or existence, life; means or manner of living) life

¤ *Physics*

Epicurus tells us that Physics is the inquiry into the nature of all things – what we today would refer to as science. Importantly, in *Epicurus'* time, physics was seen as part of philosophy, not as a separate discipline.

Remember that *Epicurus* argued that philosophy, including physics, provided the answers to the questions of how to achieve happiness. So much of his physics is directed at the previous problems that he identified and how to overcome them.

Laertius tells us:
'The physics[a] concerns the nature of all things[b]... physics is about the origin[c] and cessation[d] and the nature of things;' [Laertius, 31]

Epicurus tells us:
'And it is necessary to believe[e] that the authoritative[f] responsibility of the above (physics) is knowing accurately the business[g] of inquiring into the nature of things[h], and that happiness[i] depends on this.' [Laertius, 78]

---

[a] φυσικὸν (φυσικός physics; of or produced by nature, natural, physical) physics

[b] φύσεως (φύσις the nature of things, laws, order, of nature; nature, universe) the nature of things

[c] γενέσεως (γένεσις origin, source, creation) origin

[d] φθορᾶς (φθορά destruction, ruin, decay, cessation) cessation

[e] νομίζειν (νομίζω to hold a custom or usage, to follow as custom or usage; to deem, acknowledge, think, suppose; believe, regard) to believe

[f] κυριωτάτων (κύριος master, lord, having power or authority over; authoritative, most powerful) authoritative

[g] ἔργον work, business, employment, that with which one is occupied; an act, deed, thing done

[h] φυσιολογίας (φυσιολογία the inquiring into physics or nature or natural causes and phenomena; inquiring into the nature of things) the nature of things

[i] μακάριον (μακάριος blessed, happy, prosperous, fortunate) happiness

'If our apprehension[a] of celestial phenomena[b] and about death[c] never troubled[d] us and was not anything to us, and moreover if to not understand thoroughly the limits[e] of pains[f] and of desires[g], we would not need to inquiry into the nature of things[h].' [Laertius, Maxim XI, 142]

In the letter to Herodotus *Epicurus* provides a summary of his physics. In the letter, *Epicurus* tells us three key points that he builds upon in his ethics: everything is either material in nature or space; our psyche is material in nature and does not exist after death; and that celestial phenomena is not due to the gods

Everything is either material in nature or space
'First that nothing comes into being[i] from what is not...'
[Laertius, 38]

---

[a] ὑποψίαι (ὑποψία suspicion, ill-feeling, apprehension) apprehension

[b] μετεώρων (μετέωρος raised from the ground, in mid-air, high in the air; things in heaven above; celestial phenomena, astronomical and meteorological phenomena) celestial phenomena (such as lightening, thunder, rain, the stars, sun, moon and planets)

[c] θανάτου (θάνατος death) death

[d] ἠνώχλουν (ὀχλέω to trouble, molest, disturb) troubled

[e] ὅρους (ὅρος boundary, landmark, limit; rule, standard) limits

[f] ἀλγηδόνων (ἀλγηδών a sense of pain, pain, suffering) pains

[g] ἐπιθυμιῶν (ἐπιθυμέω upon desire, to keep the desire turned up, to set one's heart upon something, to have a desire for, to desire, covert) desires

[h] Φυσιολογίας (φυσιολογία the inquiring into physics or nature or natural causes and phenomena; the nature of things) inquire into the nature of things

[i] Γίνεται (γίνομαι to come into existence, begin to be, to come into a new state of being, born; to become, to come to pass, happen; to arise, appear; to be made) comes into being

'All is made up of material substances[a] and emptiness[b]... which we call also space[c] and immaterial[d] nature[e]' [Laertius, 39-40]

'And of the material substances some are compounds[f] and some out of which compounds are made. And these are atomic[g] and not subject to change[h]... So that atomic origins[i] are necessarily the nature of material substances[j] ' [Laertius, 40-41]

Our psyche is material in nature and does not exist after death

---

[a] σώματα (σῶμα the body of a person or animal; the dead body or corpse; in general, a body, i.e. any material or corporeal substance; the whole body of a thing) material substances

[b] κενόν (κενός empty, groundless, fruitless; void, devoid of truth, destitute; vain, without effect, lacking worth; opinion) emptiness

[c] χώραν (χώρα a space, a space in which a thing is; a place, spot) space

[d] ἀνάφη (ἀναφής impalpable, not perceptible to touch, intangible, imperceptible, incorporeal, immaterial) immaterial

[e] φύσιν (φύσις the nature of things, laws, order, of nature; nature, universe) nature

[f] συγκρίσεις (σύγκρισις aggregation, combination, compound substance, compound) compounds

[g] ἄτομα (ἄτομος atomic, that which cannot be cut in two or divided, indivisible) atomic

[h] ἀμετάβλητα (ἀμετάβλητος not subject to change, unchangeable) not subject to change

[i] ἀρχάς (ἀρχή beginning, origin, first cause) origin

[j] σωμάτων (σῶμα the body of a person or animal; the dead body or corpse; in general, a body, i.e. any material or corporeal substance; the whole body of a thing) material substances

'… the psyche[a] is a material substance[b] composed of small parts[c] abiding beside[d] the whole aggregate[e] (the body).' [Laertius, 63]

'And when the whole aggregate breaks up[f] (when the body decomposes, that is when we die), the psyche is dispersed[g] and no longer has these powers[h], and nor can it move, just as it does not possess sensations[i]' [Laertius, 65]

'Those who say the psyche[j] is incorporeal[k] speak foolishly[l].' [Laertius, 67]

---

[a] ψυχή psyche, breath, breath of life, vital force, the source of life, the life, the spirit, the soul, anima; that which is responsible for perception, thoughts, emotions, desires and affections; the mind

[b] σῶμα the body of a person or animal; the dead body or corpse; in general, a body, i.e. any material or corporeal substance; the whole body of a thing; material substance

[c] λεπτομερές (λεπτομερής small parts, composed of small parts or particles) composed of small parts

[d] παρεσπαρμένον (παραμένω to remain beside, to abide beside, stand by, continue always near) abiding beside

[e] ἄθροισμα (ἄθροισμα that which is gathered, aggregate, assemblage of atoms) aggregate (the physical body)

[f] λυομένου (λύω to lose a person or thing tied or bound, to loose, to unbind, release from bonds, set free; resolve a whole into its parts, dissolve, to break up, demolish, destroy) breaks up

[g] διασπείρεται (διασπείρω scatter or spread about, disperse) dispersed

[h] δυνάμεις (δύναμις power, strength, might, ability, faculty, capacity

[i] αἴσθησιν (αἴσθησις sense perception, sensation, the senses; perception, not only by the senses but also by the intellect, cognition) sensations

[j] ψυχήν (ψυχή psyche, breath, breath of life, vital force, the source of life, the life, the spirit, the soul, anima; that which is responsible for perception, thoughts, emotions, desires and affections; the mind) psyche

[k] ἀσώματον (ἀσώματος no body, disembodied, immaterial, incorporeal)

[l] ματαΐζουσιν (ματάζω speak or work folly, to make empty, vain, foolish) speak foolishly

Celestial phenomena are not due to the gods

'And indeed, celestial phenomena[a] - their motion[b] and turning[c] and eclipse[d] and rising[e] and setting[f] and the like - are not being administered by[g], either appointed now or in the future, those who at the same time have complete happiness[h] and incorruption[i].'
[Laertius, 76]

'Hence, from out of the original[j] retentions[k] and aggregations[l] of these in the genesis[m] of the cosmos[n] there is need to suppose that

---

[a] μετεώροις (μετέωρος raised from the ground, in mid-air, high in the air; things in heaven above; celestial phenomena, astronomical and meteorological phenomena) celestial phenomena (such as lightening, thunder, rain, the stars, sun, moon and planets)

[b] φοράν (φορά an act, carrying, gestation, bringing forth, being born or carried along, motion, motion of the celestial phenomena)

[c] τροπήν (τροπή turning; turning of celestial phenomena)

[d] ἔκλειψιν (ἔκλειψις eclipse, abandonment, failing, cessation, abandonment of Sun or Moon) eclipse

[e] ἀνατολήν (ἀνατολή rising, rising of the sun and stars; east) rising

[f] δύσιν (δύσις sinking or setting, setting of the sun and stars; west) setting

[g] λειτουργοῦντος (λειτουργέω to serve the state at one's own cost; to perform public duties; to do a service, perform, work, administer) being administered by

[h] μακαριότητα (μακάριος blessed, happy, prosperous, fortunate) happiness

[i] ἀφθαρσίας (ἀφθαρσία incorruption, purity, integrity, sincerity, incorruptness; not liable to corruption, decay, imperishable, immortality) incorruptness

[j] ἀρχῆς (ἀρχή beginning, origin, first cause; first principle, element) first principles

[k] ἐναπολήψεις (ἐναπόληψις catching, seizing or receiving in and from, catching, retention, being caught up, involved in, inclusion) retentions

[l] συστροφῶν (συστροφή twisting up together, a binding together; that which is rolled into one mass, collection, gathering; physical mass, conglomerate, aggregate) aggregations

[m] γενέσει (γένεσις genesis; origin, source; production, generation, coming into being; birth; creation, all created things) genesis

[n] κόσμου (κόσμος cosmos; an apt and harmonious arrangement; (as in) ornament, decoration; order; natural order; world order, world, universe) cosmos

the invariableness[a] of these and the cycles[b] is accomplished[c].'
[Laertius, 77]

Epicurus' Physics in essence

Central to *Epicurus'* physics, and thus to his philosophy in general, are the following notions:

 : Everything is either material in nature or space;

 : Our psyche is corporeal and does not exist after death; and

 : Celestial phenomena are not due to gods.

---

[a] ἀνάγκην (ἀνάγκη necessity, imposed, constraint, invariability; in a rare sense: calamity, distress, straits) invariableness

[b] περίοδον (περίοδος going round, marching round, flank march; way round; going around in a circle; cycle or period of time) cycle

[c] συντελεῖσθαι (συντελέω to end together, bring to an end, to end completely, finish, complete, accomplish, bring to fulfilment, to finish) to bring to fulfilment

¤ *Ethics*

Laertius tells us that *Epicurus'* ethics is the enquiry into what we should do, what we should seek and what we should avoid, and importantly what the basis for these choices are:

'…ethics[a] is about choice[b] and avoidance[c], and about life[d] and the end[e].' [Laertius, 30]

Laertius goes on to tell us that:
'Feelings[f], they say, are two, pleasure[g] and pain[h], which arise in all life and one is congenial [i] and the other hostile[j], through which is judged choice and avoidance.' [Laertius, 34]

'Two (forms of) happiness[k] can be conceived, the one the highest possible, such as that of the gods, which cannot be augmented, and

---

[a] ἠθικόν (ἠθικός ethics; of or for morals, ethical, moral) ethics

[b] αἱρετῶν (αἱρετός that may be taken or conquered; to be understood; to be chosen, elected, preferred, selected, taken) choice

[c] φευκτῶν (φευκτός to be shunned, avoided, escaped from, to flee from) avoidance

[d] βίων (βιός life; a living, means or manner of living, livelihood) life

[e] τέλους (τέλος end, termination; the fulfilment or completion of anything, its consummation, issue, result; the end to which all things relate, the aim, purpose, end-goal) end

[f] πάθη (πάθος that which happens to a person or thing, experience; passion, feeling, emotion) feelings

[g] ἡδονήν (ἡδονή enjoyment, pleasure, delight; desire for pleasure) pleasure

[h] ἀλγηδόνα (ἀλγηδών a sense of pain, pain, suffering) pain

[i] οἰκεῖον (οἰκεῖος belong to one's household; one's own; kindred; friendly, congenial) congenial

[j] ἀλλότριον (ἀλλότριος belonging to another, not one's own; foreign, strange; hostile, uncongenial) hostile

[k] εὐδαιμονίαν (εὐδαιμονία good daemon, genius, lot or fortune; prosperity, good fortune, wealth, happiness) happiness

that which is determined by the addition[a] and subtraction[b] of pleasures[c].' [Laertius, 121]

'For all we do is for the sake of us having no pain[d] and no fear[e] and, when once we have attained all this, the tempest[f] of the psyche[g] are put to an end;' [Laertius, 128]

'…we call pleasure[h] the beginning and end of the happy[i] life. This is our first and common good, and through this we make the starting-point of every choice and avoidance, and so we come back to feelings[j] as the rule[k] by which to judge[l] good[m].' [Laertius, 128 - 129]

---

[a] προσθήκην (προσθήκη an addition, something added) addition

[b] ἀφαίρεσιν (ἀφαίρεσις a taking away, carrying off, removal, abstraction) subtraction

[c] ἡδονῶν (ἡδονή enjoyment, pleasure, delight; desire for pleasure) pleasures

[d] ἀλγῶμεν (ἀλγέω to feel bodily pain, suffer; to feel pain of mind, to grieve) pain

[e] ταρβῶμεν (ταρβέω to be frightened, alarmed, terrified; to fear) fear

[f] χειμών (stormy or rainy weather, winter, a tempest; a storm of calamity

[g] ψυχῆς (ψυχή psyche, breath, breath of life, vital force, the source of life, the life, the spirit, the soul, anima; that which is responsible for perception, thoughts, emotions, desires and affections; the mind) psyche

[h] ἡδονήν (ἡδονή enjoyment, pleasure, delight; desire for pleasure) pleasure

[i] μακαρίως (μακάριος blessed, happy, prosperous, fortunate) happy

[j] πάθει (πάθος that which happens to a person or thing, experience; passion, feeling, emotion) feelings

[k] κανόνι (κανών canon; a straight rod, staff, stick or bar, esp. to keep a thing straight; a measuring rod, rule; an established principle; a rule or standard, a principle or law of investigating, judging, living, acting; logic) rule

[l] κρίνοντες (κρίνω to separate, select, choose, to decide; to be of an opinion, think; to determine, resolve; to judge) to judge

[m] ἀγαθόν (ἀγαθός good, of a good nature, brave, capable; excelling in any respect, excellent, useful) good

'Go to his (*Epicurus'*) Garden and read the motto carved there: "Stranger, here you will do well to tarry; here our highest good is pleasure." [Seneca 21][a]

Epicurus' Ethics in essence

Epicurus tells us that our feelings of pleasure and pain form the basis for all our choices.

---

[a] Seneca continues: 'The care-taker of that abode, a kindly host, will be ready for you; he will welcome you with barley-meal and serve you water also in abundance, with these words: "Have you not been well entertained?" "This garden," he says, "does not whet your appetite; it quenches it. Nor does it make you more thirsty with every drink; it slakes the thirst by a natural cure, a cure that demands no fee. This is the 'pleasure' in which I have grown old."'

¤ *Prudence*

Epicurus points out that even more important than loving wisdom (philosophy) is practical wisdom (prudence), that is, the actual application of our philosophy.

'And of all this, the beginning[a] and the greatest[b] good[c] is prudence[d]. Prudence is even more valuable than philosophy[e], because all the rest (the other virtues) spring from it.' [Laertius, 132]

---

[a] ἀρχή beginning, origin, first cause; first principle, element
[b] μέγιστον (μέγας great, big, vast, high, mighty) greatest
[c] ἀγαθόν (ἀγαθός good, of a good nature, brave, capable; excelling in any respect, excellent, useful) good
[d] φρόνησις a minding to do so and so, purpose, intention, practical wisdom, prudence, thoughtfulness, understanding, thought
[e] φιλοσοφίας (φιλοσοφία philosophy; love of wisdom) philosophy

EPICURUS' DIRECTIONS – in essence

Epicurus tells us that the way to overcome the problem of pain and to achieve happiness is to:

: Be a lover of wisdom (a philosopher) - discover the nature of ourselves and the world around, and, based on what we learn, determine what we do and what we don't do.

: Practice practical wisdom (be prudent) – just don't know but actually apply that knowledge.

EPICURUS' DIRECTIONS in essence: be a philosopher

4

EPICURUS' STRATEGIES

Knowing the problems and directions is not enough to ensure that we reach our destination. We also need to know, and implement, strategies that will help us to cope with the problems that we will encounter along the way and thus will help us to follow our directions and ultimately to help us to reach our destination, namely happiness, that state free from pain.

Epicurus tells us that from the study of philosophy we learn the strategies that we need to implement to reach our destination. After reading the last chapter, perhaps *Epicurus'* strategies are already clear.

Central to the way of *Epicurus* are four strategies:
- ¤ **Do not fear the gods;**
- ¤ **Do not fear death;**
- ¤ **Do not fear pain; and**
- ¤ **Be satisfied with simple, natural and necessary pleasures.**

'If the things which result in wildly extravagant[a] pleasures[b] ended fears[c] of the mind[d], such as about celestial phenomena[e], and death[f], and pain[g], and further, if they taught them to limit[h] their desires[i], we would not find fault with them, for they would then be filled with pleasures[j] from every side and they would have no (bodily) pain[k] or distress[l] - that is the bad[m].' [Laertius, Maxim X, 142]

'Who do you consider is better than the one who: concerning the gods[n] extols them as holy[o]; and concerning death holds no fears[p]; and

---

[a] ἀσώτους (ἄσωτος of an abandoned man, one that can not be saved; abandoned, dissolute life, profligate, prodigal, recklessly wasteful, wildly or wastefully extravagant) wildly extravagant

[b] ἡδονῶν (ἡδονή enjoyment, pleasure, delight; desire for pleasure) pleasures

[c] φόβους (φόβος fear, dread, terror) fear

[d] διανοίας (διάνοια mind, the mind as the faculty of understanding, feelings, desire; thought, intention, purpose) mind

[e] μετεώρων (μετέωρος raised from the ground, in mid-air, high in the air; things in heaven above; celestial phenomena, astronomical and meteorological phenomena) celestial phenomena (such as lightening, thunder, rain, the stars, sun, moon and planets)

[f] θανάτου (θάνατος death) death

[g] ἀλγηδόνων (ἀλγηδών a sense of pain, pain, suffering) pain

[h] πέρας extremity, bound, end, finish, limit

[i] ἐπιθυμιῶν (ἐπιθυμέω upon desire, to keep the desire turned up, to set one's heart upon something, to have a desire for, to desire, covert) desires

[j] ἡδονῶν (ἡδονή enjoyment, pleasure, delight; desire for pleasure) pleasures

[k] ἀλγοῦν (ἀλγέω to feel bodily pain, suffer; to feel pain of mind, to grieve) pain

[l] λυπούμενον (λυπέωto give pain to, to pain, distress, grieve, annoy; to be pained, grieved, distressed) distress

[m] κακόν (κακός bad, of a bad nature, not as it ought to be; base, wrong; troublesome, destructive, evil; worthless) bad

[n] θεῶν (θεός a god, goddess, deity) gods

[o] ὅσια (ὅσιος pure, holy, pious, hallowed) holy

[p] ἀφόβως (ἄφοβος no fear, dread or terror; fearless, intrepid) no fears

considers the nature of things[a] to the end[b]; and that the limit[c] of good[d] is easily attained[e] and indeed easy to secure[f] for all[g]; and of the bad[h] (knows) the duration[i] or the suffering[j] is small[k].' [Laertius, 133]

(Note: *Epicurus* includes in this list of strategies the study of nature which I have included in the directions (¤ *Physics* page 16)).

¤ Do not fear the gods

In *Physics Epicurus* tells us that celestial phenomena are not due to the gods and thus are not the basis for fearing the gods. Indeed, as the following quotations tell us, *Epicurus* tells us that no phenomenon that is incongruent with their blessed nature can be due to the gods - how can something or someone who is good, or indeed perfect, do bad? That is, *Epicurus* tells us all the bad things that we fear cannot be due to the gods and thus the gods are not to be feared.

---

[a] φύσεως (φύσις the nature of things, laws, order, of nature; nature, universe) the nature of things

[b] τέλος end, termination; the fulfilment or completion of anything, its consummation, issue, result; the end to which all things relate, the aim, purpose, end-goal

[c] πέρας extremity, bound, end, finish, limit

[d] ἀγαθῶν (ἀγαθός good, of a good nature, brave, capable; excelling in any respect, excellent, useful) good

[e] εὐσυμπλήρωτόν (εὐσυμπλήρωτος easily filled up, attained) easily attained

[f] εὐπόριστον (εὐπόριστος easy to procure, obtain, acquire, secure) easy to procure

[g] διαλαμβάνοντος (διαλαμβάνω to take or receive severally, i.e. each their share; to grasp or lay hold of seperatly; to divide) for all

[h] κακῶν (κακός bad, of a bad nature, not as it ought to be; base, wrong; troublesome, destructive, evil; worthless) bad

[i] χρόνους (χρόνος time, period, duration) duration

[j] πόνους (πόνος work, toil; the consequence of toil, distress, great trouble, suffering, pain) suffering

[k] βραχεῖς (βραχύς short time; small or little in size; few in quantity; insignificant, small, petty) small

'First know that the god[a] is an eternal[b] and blessed[c] living being[d] …
and no one should attribute that which is foreign[e] to the eternal, and
unfitting[f] to the blessed.' [Laertius, 123]

'The blessed and eternal do not have troubles[g] themselves and also
don't cause such to others, so that it is not afflicted with[h] impulses
of anger[i] or grace[j] (partiality); for all such things is to be weak[k].'
[Laertius, Maxims I, 139]

Epicurus' first strategy - in essence

Do not fear the gods because they are holy and thus un-holy acts
would be incompatible with their nature.

---

[a] θεόν (θεός a god, goddess, deity) gods

[b] ἄφθαρτον (ἄφθαρτος eternal, uncorrupted, undecaying, indestructible,
immortal) eternal

[c] μακάριον (μακάριος blessed, happy, prosperous, fortunate) blessed

[d] ζῷον living being, animal

[e] ἀλλότριον (ἀλλότριος belonging to another, not one's own; foreign,
strange; hostile, uncongenial) foreign

[f] ἀνοίκειον (ἀνοίκειος not of the family, unfitting, unreasonable, alien
to) unfitting

[g] πράγματα (πρᾶγμα that which has been done, a deed, act, an
accomplished fact; wht is being accomplished, business; affairs, state-
affairs; bad or troublesome business, trouble, annoyance) troubles

[h] συνέχεται (συνέχω to hold together; to hold completely, to be holden
with, afflicted with) afflicted with

[i] ὀργαῖς (ὀργή natural impulse, disposition, character, nature;
movement or agitation of the psyche, impulse, excite, desire, anger)
impulses

[j] χάρισι (χάρις that which affords joy, pleasure, delight, sweetness,
charm, grace, loveliness; kindness; gratitude; indebtedness) grace

[k] ἀσθενεῖ (ἀσθενέω to be weak, without strength, feeble) to be weak

¤ *Do not fear death*

In *Physics Epicurus* tells us that the psyche is corporeal and that, like all corporeal things, dissolves into its elements at death. Thus we should not fear death because after death both our body and our psyche no longer exists and thus we would sense nothing, and thus there is nothing to fear.

'Accustom yourself to believe[a] that death[b] is nothing to us, since all good[c] and bad[d] require perception[e], and death is the loss of all perception. Therefore, right knowledge of this, that death is nothing to us, makes the mortal[f] life[g] enjoyable, not by adding infinite time, but by taking away the desire for immortality[h]. For nothing in life is fearful[i] to the ones genuinely seizing that there is nothing to be fearful about in not living. Therefore foolish[j] is the one saying to fear death, not because its presence[k] will cause pain[l], but because the prospect[m] of it pains. For which causes no annoyance[n] when present,

---

[a] νομίζειν (νομίζω to hold a custom or usage, to follow as custom or usage; to deem, acknowledge, think, suppose; believe, regard) to believe

[b] θάνατον (θάνατος death) death

[c] ἀγαθόν (ἀγαθός good, of a good nature, brave, capable; excelling in any respect, excellent, useful) good

[d] κακόν (κακός bad, of a bad nature, not as it ought to be; base, wrong; troublesome, destructive, evil; worthless) bad

[e] αἰσθήσει (αἴσθησις sense perception, sensation, the senses; perception, not only by the senses but also by the intellect, cognition) perception

[f] θνητόν (θνητός liable to death, mortal) mortal

[g] ζωῆς (ζωή life, that which is possessed of vitality) life

[h] ἀθανασίας (ἀθανασία no death, immortality) immortality

[i] δεινόν (δεινός fearful, terrible, dire) fearful

[j] μάταιος devoid of force, truth, success, result, useless; without ground; vain, empty, foolish) foolish

[k] παρών (παρουσία presence, arrival, the coming) presence

[l] λυπήσει (λυπέω to cause pain, to grieve) will cause pain

[m] μέλλων (μέλλω to think of doing, intend to do, or to be about to do; to be destined or likely or about to do something) the prospect

[n] ἐνοχλεῖ (ἐνοχλέω to excite, disturbance, to trouble, annoy; to worry about; to be a trouble, a nuisance)

causes empty[a] pain[b] in the expectation[c]. Death, the horrible[d] of the bad[e], is nothing to us, since when we are, death is not present[f], and when death is present, then we are not.' [Laertius, 124 – 125]

'Death is nothing to us; for what has been dissolved into its elements[g], has no perception[h], and that which has no perception is nothing to us.' [Laertius, Maxims II, 139]

'We are born[i] only once, and not born twice; and for eternity[j] exist no longer. And you are not master[k] of tomorrow, (yet) you postpone rejoicing. Life is wasted[l] by procrastination [m], and each one of us dies[n] having been too busy[o] (for rejoicing).' [Vatican, 14]

------

[a] κενῶς (κενός empty, groundless, fruitless; void, devoid of truth, destitute; vain, without effect, lacking worth; opinion) empty

[b] λυπεῖ (λυπέω to cause pain, to grieve) causes pain

[c] προσδοκώμενον (προσδοκάω expect, think, suppose) expecting

[d] φρικωδέστατον (φρικώδης attended with shivering; that which causes shuddering or horror, awful, horrible) horrible

[e] κακῶν (κακός bad, of a bad nature, not as it ought to be; base, wrong; troublesome, destructive, evil; worthless) bad

[f] πάρεστιν (πάρειμι to be present, by or near) present

[g] διαλυθέν (διαλύω loose one from another, part asunder, to dissolve into its elements, break up; put an end to)

[h] ἀναισθητεῖ (ἀναισθητέω no perception by the senses, no sensations; no cognition) no perception

[i] γεγόναμεν (γίνομαι to come into existence, begin to be, to come into a new state of being, born; to become, to come to pass, happen; to arise, appear; to be made) we have been born

[j] αἰῶνα (αἰών age, a human lifetime, life; an unbroken age, eternity) eternity

[k] κύριος master, lord, having power or authority over; authoritative, most powerful

[l] παραπόλλυται (παραπόλλυμι destroy, consume or spend to no purpose, waste, lose) wasted

[m] μελλησμῷ (μελλησμός procrastination, indecision, putting things off) procrastination

[n] ἀποθνήσκει (ἀποθνήσκω die) die

[o] ἀσχολούμενος (ἀσχολέω to be occupied or engaged or busy; not having time for something, e.g. leisure or life; be without leisure) having been too busy

'*Epicurus* upbraids those who crave, as much as those who shrink from, death: It is absurd," he says, "to run towards death because you are tired of life, when it is your manner of life that has made you run towards death." [Seneca, 24]

Epicurus' second strategy - in essence

Do not fear death because after death we do not exist and thus sense nothing, and thus there is no pain to fear.

¤ *Do not fear pain*

Epicurus tells us to not fear pain because pain is either short in duration or low in intensity.

'Pain[a] does not linger[b] continuously[c] in the flesh[d]; but indeed, the extreme[e] (pain) is present the shortest time[f], and the solitary[g] (pain) that exceed pleasure[h] in the flesh does not last for many days... [Laertius, Maxims IV, 140]

Epicurus' third strategy - in essence

Do not fear pain because pain is either short in duration or low in intensity.

---

[a] ἀλγοῦν (ἀλγέω to feel bodily pain, suffer; to feel pain of mind, to grieve) pain

[b] χρονίζει (χρονίζω to linger, last, continue, delay, to be prolonged) linger

[c] συνεχῶς (συνεχής hold together; continuous, constant) continuous

[d] σαρκί (σάρξ flesh, flesh of a living body, the body; a living creature) flesh

[e] ἄκρον (ἄκρος highest, extreme; at the farthest point, topmost) extreme

[f] χρόνον (χρόνος time; period; lifetime, age) time

[g] μόνον (μόνος alone, left alone, solitary, only, merely) solitary

[h] ἡδόμενον (ἥδομαι enjoy oneself, take one's pleasure)

¤ *Be satisfied with simple, natural and necessary pleasures*

In *Ethics Epicurus* tells us that our feelings of pleasure and pain form the basis for all our choices. But as *Epicurus* tells us below, it isn't as simple as seeking pleasure and avoiding pain.

Pleasure is the goal of the happy life

'...we call pleasure[a] the beginning[b] and goal[c] of the happy[d] life. This is our first and common good, and through this we make the starting-point of every choice[e] and avoidance[f], and so we come back to feelings[g] as the rule[h] by which to judge[i] good[j].' [Laertius, 128 - 129]

In short *Epicurus* tells us to:
: Seek pleasure (and avoid pain).

-----

[a] ἡδονήν (ἡδονή enjoyment, pleasure, delight; desire for pleasure) pleasure
[b] ἀρχὴν (ἀρχή beginning, origin, first cause) beginning
[c] τέλος end, termination; the fulfilment or completion of anything, its consummation, issue, result; the end to which all things relate, the aim, purpose, end-goal
[d] μακαρίως (μακάριος blessed, happy, prosperous, fortunate) happy
[e] αἱρέσεως (αἵρεσις act of taking, capturing; choice, that which is chosen) choice
[f] φυγῆς (φυγή flight or escape, aversion, avoidance) avoidance
[g] πάθει (πάθος that which happens to a person or thing, experience; passion, feeling, emotion) feelings
[h] κανόνι (κανών canon; a straight rod, staff, stick or bar, esp. to keep a thing straight; a measuring rod, rule; an established principle; a rule or standard, a principle or law of investigating, judging, living, acting; logic) rule
[i] κρίνοντες (κρίνω to separate, select, choose, to decide; to be of an opinion, think; to determine, resolve; to judge) to judge
[j] ἀγαθόν (ἀγαθός good, of a good nature, brave, capable; excelling in any respect, excellent, useful) good

BUT don't choose all pleasures, and don't avoid all pains

Epicurus tells us that before we choose to satisfy a pleasure or avoid a pain, we need to consider the consequences of our choice. For example, we need to consider the negatives that may result from satisfying a particular pleasure, and the positives that may result from accepting a particular pain.

'For we know this (pleasure) is our first and innate[a] good[b], and because of this we do not choose every pleasure, but pass over[c] many pleasures[d] when more unpleasant[e] things follow from them. And many pains[f] we consider better than pleasures whenever large pleasures follow... Therefore, while all natural pleasures are good, not all however are chosen; and while all pains are bad, not all is to be avoided.' [Laertius, 129]

'When we say that pleasure[g] is to be the goal[h], we do not mean profligate[i] pleasures or the enjoyments[j] of lying down[k], as some

---

[a] σύμφυτον (σύμφυτος born together, born with, congenital or hereditary, innate) common

[b] ἀγαθόν (ἀγαθός good, of a good nature, brave, capable; excelling in any respect, excellent, useful) good

[c] ὑπερβαίνομεν (ὑπερβαίνω step over, pass beyond, pass up, pass over) pass over

[d] ἡδονήν (ἡδονή enjoyment, pleasure, delight; desire for pleasure) pleasure

[e] δυσχερές (δυσχερής hard to take in hand, annoying, difficult, unpleasant)

[f] ἀλγηδόνας (ἀλγηδών a sense of pain, pain, suffering) pain

[g] ἡδονήν (ἡδονή enjoyment, pleasure, delight; desire for pleasure) pleasure

[h] τέλος end, termination; the fulfilment or completion of anything, its consummation, issue, result; the end to which all things relate, the aim, purpose, end-goal

[i] ἀσώτων (ἄσωτος of an abandoned man, one that can not be saved; abandoned, dissolute life, profligate, prodigal, recklessly wasteful, wildly or wastefully extravagant) profligate

[j] ἀπολαύσει (ἀπόλαυσις act of enjoying, fruition, pleasure) enjoyment

[k] κειμένας (κεῖμαι to lie, to lie outstretched, to lie down to rest, repose) lying down

think in ignorance and disagreement or wrongly accept; but rather the (goal) is no pain[a] in the body[b] and no turmoil[c] in the psyche[d]. For it is not continuous drinking and of revelry, and not the enjoyment of ... women, and not an extravagant table bearing large amounts of fish and other things, which produce a pleasant life; but it is calm and collected[e] reasoning[f], and searching out[g] the reasons[h] of every choice[i] and avoidance[j], and banishing those beliefs[k] through which the greatest turmoils[l] take possession of the psyche[m].' [Laertius, 131-132]

---

[a] ἀλγεῖν (ἀλγέω to feel bodily pain, suffer; to feel pain of mind, to grieve) feeling pain

[b] σῶμα body, the body of a person; any material substance; the whole body of a thing

[c] ταράττεσθαι (ταράσσω to agitate, to stir up trouble, turmoil, to takeaway calmness of mind, to make restless, to throw into disorder) turmoil

[d] ψυχήν (ψυχή psyche, breath, breath of life, vital force, the source of life, the life, the spirit, the soul, anima; that which is responsible for perception, thoughts, emotions, desires and affections; the mind) psyche

[e] νήφων to be sober, to be calm and collected, dispassionate, circumspect

[f] λογισμός reason, reasoning power; reckoning, calculation, computation, consideration

[g] ἐξερευνῶν (ἐξερευνάω search out or examine anxiously and diligently) searching out

[h] αἰτίας (αἰτία responsibility; cause, reason, grounds; charge of crime) reasons

[i] αἱρέσεως (αἵρεσις act of taking, capturing; choice, that which is chosen) choice

[j] φυγῆς (φυγή flight or escape, aversion, avoidance) avoidance

[k] δόξας (δόξα opinion, judgement, view, a notion, belief, thought, expectation; splendour, brightness, magnificence, excellence, majesty, exalted) beliefs

[l] θόρυβος a loud confused noise, tumult, uproar, turmoil, confusion

[m] ψυχάς (ψυχή psyche, breath, breath of life, vital force, the source of life, the life, the spirit, the soul, anima; that which is responsible for perception, thoughts, emotions, desires and affections; the mind) psyche

'With all desires[a] one must ask this question[b]: what will happen to me if the desire one was seeking was satisfied[c]; and what if it was not satisfied?' [Vatican, 71]

In short *Epicurus* tells us to:
: Seek pleasures, but don't seek to satisfy those pleasures that result in greater pain.
: Avoid pains, but don't avoid those pains that result in greater pleasure.

Further, only some desires are natural and necessary

Epicurus tells us that some desires are natural and some based only on empty opinion, and that we need to satisfy only our natural desires to achieve happiness. But, he goes on to tell us that not all natural desires need be satisfied for our happiness.

'We must reflect that of desires[d] some are natural[e], others are empty[f]; and that of the natural some are necessary[g], and some natural only. And of the necessary some are necessary for happiness[h], and

---

[a] ἐπιθυμίας (ἐπιθυμία desire, craving, longing after a thing, yearning) desires

[b] ἐπερώτημα a question, an inquiry; a demand; earnest seeking

[c] τελεσθῆ (τελέω to bring to a close, to finish, to end, to complete, accomplish, execute, achieve) satisfied

[d] ἐπιθυμιῶν (ἐπιθυμέω upon desire, to keep the desire turned up, to set one's heart upon something, to have a desire for, to desire, covert) desires

[e] φυσικαί (φυσικός physics; of or produced by nature, natural, of or to do with physical things) natural

[f] κεναί (κενός empty, groundless, fruitless; void, devoid of truth, destitute; vain, without effect, lacking worth; opinion) empty

[g] ἀναγκαίων (ἀνάγκη necessity, imposed, constraint; in a rare sense: calamity, distress, straits) necessary

[h] εὐδαιμονίαν (εὐδαιμονία good daemon, genius, lot or fortune; prosperity, good fortune, wealth, happiness) happiness

some in order that the body[a] is free from trouble, and some for life[b] itself.' [Laertius, 127]

'Of desires, some are natural and necessary; and some natural but not necessary; and some neither natural nor necessary, but occurring due to empty[c] opinion[d]. [Laertius, added by someone in antiquity: *Epicurus* regards as natural and necessary those which releases us from pain, such as drink[e] when thirsty[f]; and natural and not necessary those which only vary the pleasure[g] without taking away the pain[h], such as extravagant[i] foods[j]; and neither natural nor necessary such as crowns[k] and the erection of statues[l].] [Laertius, Maxims XXIX, 149]

For example, the desire for simple food (hunger) if not fulfilled leads to pain and therefore is a necessary natural desire, whereas the desire to have extravagant food if not fulfilled does not result in pain and therefore is an unnecessary desire.

---

[a] Σώματος (σῶμα body, the body of a person; any material substance; the whole body of a thing) body

[b] ζῆν (ζωη life, state of one filled with breath or vitality; existence; a way of life, a living, one's means of life) life

[c] κενήν (κενός empty, groundless, fruitless; void, devoid of truth, destitute; vain, without effect, lacking worth; opinion) empty

[d] δόξαν (δόξα opinion, judgement, view, a notion, belief, thought, expectation; splendour, brightness, magnificence, excellence, majesty, exalted) beliefs

[e] ποτόν (ποτός drink) drink

[f] δίψους (δίψος thirst) thirsty

[g] ἡδονήν (ἡδονή enjoyment, pleasure, delight; desire for pleasure) pleasure

[h] ἄλγημα pain felt or caused, suffering

[i] πολυτελῆ (πολυτελέω to be extravagant, expensive, costly) extravagant

[j] σιτία (σιτίον corn, grain; food made form grain, bread; food, provisions) foods

[k] στεφάνους (στέφανος that which surrounds; a crown) crown

[l] ἀνδριάντων (ἀνδριάς image of a man, statue) statue

In short *Epicurus* tells us:
: For happiness only some of our natural desires need be satisfied.

Natural and necessary desires are easy to satisfy

'... and that whatever is natural[a] is easy to procure[b] and only the empty[c] is difficult to procure[d].' [Laertius, 130]

'Nature's[e] wealth[f] is defined[g] and is easy to procure; but the wealth of empty[h] opinions[i] fails into infinity.' [Laertius, Maxims XV, 144]

'He who understands the limits[j] of life[k] knows how easy it is to obtain enough to remove the pains[l] of want[m] and make the whole of

---

[a] φυσικόν (φυσικός physics; of or produced by nature, natural, of or to do with physical things) natural

[b] εὐπόριστον (εὐπόριστος easy to procure, acquire, gain or secure) easy to procure

[c] κενόν (κενός empty, groundless, fruitless; void, devoid of truth, destitute; vain, without effect, lacking worth; opinion) empty

[d] δυσπόριστον (δυσπόριστος difficult to procure, acquire, gain or secure) difficult to procure

[e] φύσεως (φύσις the nature of things, laws, order, of nature; nature, universe) nature's

[f] πλοῦτος wealth, riches, abundance, plenitude

[g] ὥρισται (ὁρίζω to define, to mark out the boundaries or limits, bound; to determine, ordain, appoint) is defined

[h] κενῶν (κενός empty, groundless, fruitless; void, devoid of truth, destitute; vain, without effect, lacking worth; opinion) empty

[i] δοξῶν (δόξα opinion, judgement, view, a notion, belief, thought, expectation; splendour, brightness, magnificence, excellence, majesty, exalted) opinions

[j] πέρατα (πέρας extremity, bound, end, finish, limit) limits

[k] βίου (βίος the period or course of life or existence, life; means or manner of living) life

[l] ἀλγοῦν (ἀλγέω to feel bodily pain, suffer; to feel pain of mind, to grieve) pains

[m] ἔνδειαν (ἔνδεια want, need, lack, deficiency, defect) want

life complete and perfect[a]. So that not one want[b] involving anxious[c] circumstances[d] do we need to get for ourselves.' [Laertius, Maxims XXI, 146]

'Among natural[e] desires[f] those not leading to pain when not fulfilled[g], (and) involving intense effort[h], are also due to empty[i] opinion[j] - if they are not dissolved[k] it is not because of their own nature[l], but because of the empty opinions of humans. [Laertius, Maxim XXX, 149]

In short *Epicurus* tells us:
 : Natural desires are easy to satisfy;
 : Unnatural, empty desires are difficult to satisfy.

---

[a] παντελῆ (παντελής all-complete, perfect, completely, perfectly, utterly) complete and perfect

[b] προσδεῖται (προσδέω to need besides or in addition; to be in want of, stand in need of besides; bind on or to, attach) want

[c] ἀγῶνας (ἀγών a gathering, a place of assembly; a place of contest, a contest; mental struggle, anxiety) anxiety

[d] πραγμάτων (πρᾶγμα deed, act, that which has been done; a matter, affair; thing of consequence, importance; circumstances, affairs) circumstances

[e] φυσικῶν (φυσικός physics; of or produced by nature, natural, of or to do with physical things) natural

[f] ἐπιθυμιῶν (ἐπιθυμέω upon desire, to keep the desire turned up, to set one's heart upon something, to have a desire for, to desire, covert) desires

[g] συντελεσθῶσιν (συντελέω to end together; to end completely, bring to an end, bring to fulfilment, complete, finish; to be caused, brought about) fulfilled

[h] σπουδή haste, speed; zeal, pains, trouble, effort

[i] κενήν (κενός empty, groundless, fruitless; void, devoid of truth, destitute; vain, without effect, lacking worth) empty

[j] δόξαν (δόξα opinion, judgement, view, a notion, belief, thought, expectation; splendour, brightness, magnificence, excellence, majesty, exalted) beliefs

[k] διαχέονται (διαχέω scatter, dispersed, dissolved; to become diffused or relaxed)

[l] φύσιν (φύσις the nature of things, laws, order, of nature; nature, universe) nature

Be satisfied with simple, natural and necessary pleasures

'We regard self-sufficiency[a] as a great good[b], not in order to always use little, but so that we may be satisfied[c] with little if perchance we don't have much... Simple[d] flavours[e] bring equal pleasure[f] as a costly[g] way of living[h], when once the pain[i] of want[j] has been removed' [Laertius, 130]

'Contented poverty is an honourable estate.' [Seneca, 2]

Seneca comments: 'Indeed, if it be contented, it is not poverty at all. It is not the man who has too little, but the man who craves more, that is poor.' [Seneca, 2]

'Whoever does not regard what he has as most ample wealth, is unhappy, though he be master of the whole world.' [Seneca, 9]

'If you live according to nature, you will never be poor; if you live according to opinion, you will never be rich' [Seneca, 16]

---

[a] αὐτάρκειαν (αὐτάρκεια self-sufficiency in oneself, independence) self-sufficiency

[b] ἀγαθόν (ἀγαθός good, of a good nature, brave, capable; excelling in any respect, excellent, useful) good

[c] ἀρκώμεθα (ἀρκέω suffice, be enough, ward off, keep off a thing from a person; to be strong enough, to be sufficient, to be satisfied, to be contented) satisfied

[d] λιτοί (λιτός simple, inexpensive, frugal, plain; paltry, petty, small) simple

[e] χυλοί (χυλός juice, barley water, gruel; flavour, taste) flavours

[f] ἡδονήν (ἡδονή enjoyment, pleasure, delight; desire for pleasure) pleasure

[g] πολυτελεῖ (πολυτελής very expensive, costly, lavish, extravagant) costly

[h] διαίτῃ (δίαιτα way of living, mode of life; dwelling, abode) way of living

[i] ἀλγοῦν (ἀλγέω to feel bodily pain, suffer; to feel pain of mind, to grieve) pain

[j] ἔνδειαν (ἔνδεια want, want of means, poverty, lack, need, deficiency, defect) want

Seneca continues: 'Nature's wants are slight; the demands of opinion are boundless.' [Seneca, 16]

'If you wish to make Pythocles rich do not add to his store of money, but subtract from his desires.' [Seneca, 21]

'Poverty[a], if measured by the goal[b] of nature[c], is great wealth[d]; but wealth, if not limited[e], is great poverty.' [Vatican, 25]

'The cry[f] of the flesh[g]: not to hunger[h], not to thirst[i], and not to be cold[j]; those having these and expect to have them, contend with the above (the gods) for happiness[k].' [Vatican, 33]

'Nothing is enough[l] to whom enough is little[m].' [Vatican, 68]

In short *Epicurus* tells us to:
: Be satisfied with simple, natural and necessary pleasures – they are all that are really necessary for a happy life and they are easy to obtain; and

---

[a] πενία poverty, need, lack

[b] τέλει (τέλος end, termination; the fulfilment or completion of anything, its consummation, issue, result; the end to which all things relate, the aim, purpose, end-goal) goal

[c] φύσεως (φύσις the nature of things, laws, order, of nature; nature, universe) nature

[d] πλοῦτος wealth, riches, abundance, plenitude

[e] ὁριζόμενος (ὁρίζω to define, to mark out the boundaries or limits, bound; to determine, ordain, appoint) limited

[f] φωνή a sound, tone, the sound of the voice; the voice or cry of animals

[g] σαρκός (σάρξ flesh, flesh of a living body, the body; a living creature) flesh

[h] πεινῆν (πεῖνα hunger famine; hunger or longing for a thing) hunger

[i] διψῆν (δίψα thirst; thirst for) thirst

[j] ῥιγοῦν (ῥῖγος cold, frost; shivering) cold

[k] εὐδαιμονίας (εὐδαιμονία good daemon, genius, lot or fortune; prosperity, good fortune, wealth, happiness) happiness

[l] ἱκανὸν (ἱκανός sufficient, enough, adequate) enough

[m] ὀλίγον (ὀλίγος little, small, few) little

: Do not be anxious about not having extravagant, empty and unnecessary pleasures – they are unnecessary for a happy life and cause most of our pains of want (the pains they cause when trying to obtain them, and the pains we feel when we don't have them).

Epicurus' fourth strategy - in essence

: Seek pleasures, but don't seek to satisfy those pleasures that result in greater pain.
: Avoid pains, but don't avoid those pains that result in greater pleasure.
: Be satisfied with simple, natural and necessary pleasures.
: Do not be anxious about not having extravagant, empty and unnecessary pleasures.

EPICURUS' STRATEGIES – in essence

Central to the way of *Epicurus* are four strategies:

¤ **Do not fear the gods** – because they wouldn't do anything unholy

¤ **Do not fear death** – because after death we do not exist and thus sense nothing

¤ **Do not fear pain** – because pain is either short in duration or low in intensity

¤ **Be satisfied with simple, natural and necessary pleasures** – because they are all we need for a happy life (and seeking other pleasures results in pain).

THE WAY OF EPICURUS – a summary

THE DESTINATION - happiness
¤ Happiness – a healthy body and tranquil mind

PROBLEMS
¤ Fear of the gods
¤ Fear of death
¤ Fear of pain itself
¤ Pains of want

EPICURUS' DIRECTIONS - be a philosophy
¤ Be a lover of wisdom (a philosopher)
¤ Practice practical wisdom (prudence)

EPICURUS' STRATEGIES
¤ Do not fear the gods
¤ Do not fear death
¤ Do not fear pain
¤ Be satisfied with simple, natural and necessary pleasures

THE WAY OF EPICURUS – in essence

¤ Seek a healthy body and tranquil mind
¤ Be a philosopher
¤ Be satisfied with simple, natural and necessary pleasures

Bibliography

Gummere, R. M. (1917 - 1925) translation of Lucius Annaeus
Seneca's *Moral Epistles,* The Loeb Classical Library.
Cambridge, Mass.: Harvard UP, 1917-25. 3 vols –
sourced from:
http://www.stoics.com/seneca_epistles_book_1.html

Inwood, B. & Gerson, L.P. (1994) *The Epicurus Reader – Selected
Writings and Testimonia.* Indianapolis: Hackett
Publishing Company.

Hicks, R.D. (1925) translation of Diogenes Laertius' *Lives of
Eminent Philosophers.* Loeb Classical Library –
sourced from: *http://www.perseus.tufts.edu/.*

Liddell and Scott, (1889) *An intermediate Greek-English Lexicon.*
Oxford: Oxford University Press.

Liddell, Scott and Jones *Greek English Lexicon* – sourced from
http://www.perseus.tufts.edu

Saint-Andre, P. (2010) *Vatican Sayings by Epicurus* sourced from:
*http://www.monadnock.net/Epicurus /vatican-
sayings.html#n4*

Thayer, J.H., (1885) *The New Thayer's Greek-English Lexicon of
the New Testament.* Peabody, Massachusetts:
Hendrickson Publishers.

Yonge, C.D. (1853) translation of Diogenes Laertius' *The Lives
and Opinions of Eminent Philosophers* (Kindle
Version)

About the author

One of **Gary's** passions is to explore the mind and what shapes it. In the series, *Ways of the World* Gary explores different ways of the world that have helped to shape his mind – including religious, philosophical and secular ways. Books in this series currently include: *Exploring the Way of Epictetus, Exploring the Way of the Buddha, Exploring the Way of Lao Tzu, Exploring the Way of Jesus,* and this book *Exploring the Way of Epicurus.* Other ways that have influenced Gary include science, psychology, engineering, philosophy, and more broadly, Western Culture.

Gary's other passions include: Cheryl (who he has had the great joy of being married to for more than forty years); their children and grandchildren; exploring a good life and wisdom (what they are and how to achieve them); reading (especially about philosophy, religions, science, psychology, technology, health and fitness…); running, health and fitness - and coffee with Cheryl.

Gary has tertiary qualifications in engineering, science (cognitive psychology) and religious studies.

Gary is also the author of:
Exploring the Way of the Buddha
Exploring the Way of Epictetus
Exploring the Way of Jesus
Exploring the Way of Lao Tzu
The Way of Sophia with Humps in Mind
Exploring a Good Life with Humps in Mind
Exploring Wisdom with Humps in Mind
Exploring the Mind - Discovering Humps and How they shape us
Gary and Cheryl are the authors of:
The Way of Sophia circa 2017
Exploring a Way to a Good Life
Exploring Wisdom

Made in the USA
San Bernardino, CA
10 February 2018